RAYMOND SMITH

Unstoppable

A 13-Week Journey to Living in Step with the Power of the Holy Spirit

DISCIPLE
BLUEPRINT
PRESS

Contents

1

Introduction to the Holy Spirit Bible Study

Why Study the Holy Spirit?

The Holy Spirit is often the most misunderstood member of the Trinity. While much emphasis is placed on God the Father and Jesus Christ, the Holy Spirit's role in creation, salvation, and the believer's daily life is sometimes overlooked. Yet, without the Spirit, there is no conviction of sin, no regeneration, no spiritual growth, and no power for Christian living.

This study is designed to provide a comprehensive understanding of the Holy Spirit's nature, work, and impact on our lives. Over the course of thirteen weeks, we will journey through the Scriptures, exploring the Holy Spirit's role in the Old Testament, His presence in the life of Jesus, and His transformative power in believers today.

The Structure of This Study

This study is divided into three key sections:

Part 1: Foundations (Weeks 1-4)

- **Who is the Holy Spirit?** Understanding His deity, personality, and role in the Trinity.
- **The Holy Spirit in the Old Testament.** His role in creation, prophecy, empowerment, and guidance.
- **The Holy Spirit in the Life of Jesus.** From conception to resurrection, the Spirit's work in Christ's ministry.
- **The Role of the Holy Spirit in Salvation.** Conviction, regeneration, adoption, and assurance.

Part 2: The Holy Spirit and the Believer (Weeks 5-9)

- **The Indwelling of the Holy Spirit.** What it means for the Spirit to live within us.
- **The Baptism of the Holy Spirit.** Examining theological perspectives and scriptural truths.
- **The Fruit of the Holy Spirit.** Character transformation through the Spirit (Galatians 5:22-23).
- **The Role of the Holy Spirit in Sanctification.** Growing in holiness through the Spirit's work.
- **The Holy Spirit in Prayer.** How the Spirit intercedes and teaches us to pray (Romans 8:26).

Part 3: The Holy Spirit and Spiritual Living (Weeks 10-13)

- **The Holy Spirit and Spiritual Warfare.** Relying on the Spirit's power to resist the enemy.
- **Hearing and Listening for the Holy Spirit.** Learning discernment and recognizing His voice.
- **Walking in the Holy Spirit.** Living daily under the Spirit's leadership.
- **The Holy Spirit and the Church.** His empowerment for

mission, unity, and spiritual gifts.

How to Use This Study

Each lesson follows a structured format designed for depth and clarity:

1. **Introduction:** Provides an illustration, historical context, and theological background.
2. **Goals of the Lesson:** Clearly defined learning objectives.
3. **Introduction Questions:** Thought-provoking questions to assess prior understanding.
4. **Key Scriptures:** A detailed breakdown of scriptural truths, including linguistic insights and cross-references.
5. **Summary:** A collective teaching of key scriptures and overarching themes.
6. **Application:** Practical steps for applying the lesson.
7. **Reflection Questions:** Questions to help internalize the lesson's impact.
8. **Prayer Prompt:** A guided prayer using the ACTS method (Adoration, Confession, Thanksgiving, Supplication).

Expectations for This Study

- **Commit to studying each lesson thoughtfully.** Take time to read, reflect, and pray over the material.
- **Engage with the reflection questions.** This study is not just about gaining knowledge but about transformation.
- **Seek the Holy Spirit's guidance.** As you progress, ask the Spirit to reveal His truth to you in a personal way.
- **Apply what you learn.** The Spirit's work is meant to be lived out in our daily lives.

A Prayer for This Journey

Heavenly Father, thank You for the gift of the Holy Spirit. As I begin this study, open my heart and mind to understand Your Spirit's role in my life. Teach me to walk in step with Him, to recognize His voice, and to rely on His power. Transform me from the inside out, that I may grow in faith and obedience. In Jesus' name, Amen.

2

Lesson 1: Who is the Holy Spirit?

Key Truth:

The Holy Spirit isn't a mystery to fear—He's a person to know, a presence to trust, and a power to live by.

Section 1: Introduction

Illustration:

Imagine standing before a massive construction site with workers moving efficiently, but an unseen force is orchestrating their tasks. Though you don't see the architect, his influence is undeniable—his plans guide the workers, his instructions shape the outcome.

Now imagine trying to navigate your life without knowing the voice of the One guiding your every step. You wouldn't trust a GPS that refused to speak or a coach who never stepped onto the field. So why do so many Christians ignore the Holy Spirit—the very presence Jesus promised would lead, teach, and empower us?

Personal Connection:

Maybe you've heard the name "Holy Spirit" your whole life... but you've never really been taught what that means. Maybe the idea makes you nervous, confused, or unsure. If so, you're not alone. But this lesson will help you discover that the Holy Spirit isn't weird or optional—He's essential.

In-Depth Background:

The Holy Spirit is often misunderstood. Some imagine Him as a vague force, others as an emotional experience. But Scripture reveals that the Holy Spirit is a divine person—co-equal with the Father and the Son, fully God, and fully active in the life of every believer.

Understanding who the Holy Spirit is lays the foundation for everything else in this study. If we don't know who He is, we won't recognize His voice, trust His power, or rely on His presence.

A Personal Example:

I once sat with a young woman in our church who had followed Jesus for years but confessed she still thought of the Holy Spirit as some vague "power source" she occasionally tapped into. She said, "I never thought of Him as someone I could actually know." When she began reading the Gospels and saw how Jesus described the Spirit—as Comforter, Teacher, Friend—it clicked. "For the first time," she said, "I realized I was never alone. He's with me. In me. Not just a force, but a friend."

Section 2: Goals of the Lesson

By the end of this lesson, students will:

1. Understand that the Holy Spirit is a person, not a force—equal with the Father and Son.
2. Recognize the Spirit's divine nature and role in creation, salvation, and daily life.
3. Correct common misconceptions and learn how to relate to the Spirit personally.
4. Begin building a biblical foundation for Spirit-filled living.

Section 3: Introduction Questions

Who is the Holy Spirit?

Many people think of the Holy Spirit as a force or energy, but Scripture teaches He is a divine person—the third Person of the Trinity. He has emotions, a will, speaks, and interacts personally with believers.

Why do so many people misunderstand the Holy Spirit?

Cultural confusion, limited teaching, and fear of the supernatural can all contribute. Clarifying who He is biblically helps

7

remove that uncertainty.

How do you feel about your relationship with the Holy Spirit right now?

This reflection opens the door to honesty and growth. There's no shame in saying "I'm not sure"—that's exactly why this study exists.

Section 4: Key Scriptures

Genesis 1:2

From the opening verses of Scripture, the Holy Spirit is active in creation, hovering over the waters—bringing order, life, and purpose.

- **The Spirit's Role in Creation** – Not a passive observer, the Spirit is God's creative power in motion.
- **Ruach Elohim** – The Hebrew word for Spirit (*ruach*) also means wind or breath, symbolizing movement and life.
- **Unity with the Trinity** – The Spirit is not a New Testament innovation but active from the very beginning.

Reflection Questions:

Q1. What does the Spirit's presence in creation reveal about His nature?

Q2. How does this change your understanding of when and where the Spirit began His work?

Matthew 28:19

Jesus instructs His disciples to baptize in the name of the Father, the Son, and the Holy Spirit—placing the Spirit on equal ground with the other two members of the Trinity.

- **The Trinity in Unity** – One name, three persons—Father, Son, and Spirit.
- **The Spirit's Authority** – This command affirms the Spirit's divine status and essential role in salvation.
- **Mission and Empowerment** – We're not only saved by the Spirit but also sent by Him.

Reflection Questions:

Q1. Why is it important that the Spirit is mentioned in Jesus' final instructions?

Q2. How does this verse reinforce the idea of the Spirit as divine?

Acts 5:3-4

Peter confronts Ananias for lying to the Holy Spirit, then clarifies, "You have not lied to men but to God."

- **The Spirit is God** – This passage removes any doubt—the Holy Spirit is not an "it" but God Himself.
- **Moral Authority** – The Spirit sees and responds to the heart.
- **Conviction and Purity** – The Spirit is actively working to keep the Church holy.

Reflection Questions:

Q1. How does this verse confirm the Spirit's divinity?

Q2. What does this reveal about the Spirit's role in our integrity and daily living?

John 14:16-17

Jesus promises a Helper who will dwell with us forever.

- **Parakletos** – Greek for Advocate, Counselor, Comforter.
- **Permanent Presence** – The Spirit is not a visitor but a permanent resident.
- **Spirit of Truth** – He teaches, reveals, and illuminates God's truth.

Reflection Questions:

Q1. How does the idea of the Spirit as your Helper change your view of His role?

Q2. What comfort do you find in knowing the Spirit dwells with you permanently?

John 16:13-14

Jesus says the Spirit will guide us into all truth and glorify Him.

- **The Spirit Speaks** – He doesn't act independently, but communicates God's will.
- **Guidance and Truth** – He leads us not just to knowledge, but into action.
- **Glorifying Christ** – The Spirit's mission is to make Jesus known.

Reflection Questions:

Q1. How can you become more sensitive to the Spirit's guidance?

Q2. In what ways does the Spirit help you glorify Jesus?

1 Corinthians 2:10-11

Paul explains that the Spirit searches the deep things of God and reveals them to us.

- **The Spirit Knows God Intimately** – He understands God's

heart and desires.
- **Revealer of Truth** – What we can't know on our own, the Spirit makes known.
- **Divine Partnership** – We aren't meant to guess at God's will—we're meant to hear it.

Reflection Questions:

Q1. Why is it encouraging to know the Spirit reveals God's heart?

Q2. How does this shape your expectations in prayer and study?

Romans 8:9

Anyone who belongs to Christ has the Spirit of God living in them.

- **The Indwelling Spirit** – Every believer receives the Spirit at salvation.
- **Belonging and Identity** – The Spirit marks us as God's own.
- **Power and Presence** – You are never alone, never abandoned.

Reflection Questions:

Q1. How does this verse define what it means to be a Christian?

Q2. How does knowing the Spirit lives in you impact your daily life?

Section 5: Summary

The Holy Spirit is not an optional part of the Christian life—He is essential. From the moment of creation to the moment of your salvation, the Spirit has been active. He is not a force, a symbol, or a fleeting presence—He is God, dwelling in you, guiding you into truth, and transforming you to look more like Christ.

Don't just study this lesson—respond to it. Ask the Spirit to reveal Himself to you in a new way. Begin this study with a prayer: "Holy Spirit, help me to know You."

Section 6: Application

- **Pray** – Ask the Holy Spirit to help you understand Him more deeply.
- **Reflect** – Consider how your view of the Spirit has been shaped by past teaching.
- **Journal** – Write down any questions you have about the Spirit.
- **Practice Awareness** – Pay attention this week to moments when you sense conviction, encouragement, or direction—and ask: Could this be the Spirit speaking?

Section 7: Reflection Questions

What did you learn about the Holy Spirit that surprised or challenged you?

How has your perception of the Holy Spirit changed through this lesson?

What would it look like for you to live each day with awareness of the Spirit's presence?

Section 8: Prayer Prompt (ACTS Model)

Adoration – Holy Spirit, You are fully God—eternal, powerful, present from the beginning. I worship You as my Guide, my Comforter, and my Helper.

Confession – Forgive me for the ways I've misunderstood or ignored You. Forgive my fear of surrendering control.

Thanksgiving – Thank You for living in me, for guiding me into truth, for always pointing me to Jesus.

Supplication – Teach me to hear Your voice more clearly. Help me walk in step with You. Make me sensitive to Your conviction and open to Your guidance.

Example Prayer:

Holy Spirit, I welcome You. I don't want to just know *about* You—I want to know You. Help me hear Your voice, recognize Your leading, and walk in Your power. Thank You for never leaving me and for always pointing me to Jesus. Amen.

3

Lesson 2: The Holy Spirit in the Old Testament

Key Truth:

The Holy Spirit wasn't absent in the Old Testament—He was already preparing hearts, empowering leaders, and revealing God's plan.

Section 1: Introduction

Illustration:

Imagine standing before a massive construction site—blueprints unrolled, builders in place—but the architect remains behind the scenes. You never see him, but everything is shaped by his plan. This is how the Holy Spirit worked throughout the Old Testament. Though His presence wasn't always front and center, His fingerprints are on every chapter of God's unfolding story.

Personal Connection:

Many Christians think of the Holy Spirit as arriving in Acts 2—as if He took the stage late in the story. But that's a misunderstanding. The Spirit was already active in creation, prophecy, leadership, and redemption from the beginning. This lesson helps us trace His movements and understand His eternal role in God's plan.

In-Depth Background:

The Hebrew word for Spirit, *ruach*, means "breath" or "wind," reflecting the Spirit's life-giving and active nature. In the Old Testament, the Spirit's work was often temporary—coming upon people for specific tasks, rather than indwelling them permanently as in the New Testament. Yet His influence was essential in shaping leaders, prophets, and events that foreshadowed Christ.

A Personal Example:

A few years ago, I taught a Bible study where one of the most faithful attendees—a man in his 60s—came up afterward looking stunned. He said, "I've read the Old Testament my whole life and somehow never realized the Holy Spirit was in it." When we revisited the story of Gideon together, it hit him: "So the Spirit was empowering people long before Acts 2?" he asked. That moment flipped a switch. He said it gave him a deeper appreciation for God's consistency—and a greater confidence that the same Spirit working in the past is still working in him today.

Section 2: Goals of the Lesson

By the end of this lesson, students will:

1. Recognize the Holy Spirit's role in creation, revelation, and empowerment.
2. Understand how the Spirit empowered individuals temporarily for specific divine purposes.
3. See the continuity between the Spirit's work in the Old and New Testaments.
4. Correct misconceptions about the Spirit being absent before Pentecost.

Section 3: Introduction Questions

Was the Holy Spirit active before Pentecost?

Yes. From creation in Genesis to prophecy in Ezekiel, the Spirit was deeply involved. His role differed from New Testament times, but His power and purpose remained.

How did the Holy Spirit work differently in the Old Testament?

He came upon individuals temporarily to empower them for specific missions—leading, delivering, or speaking God's Word.

Why does understanding the Spirit's role in the Old Testament matter today?

It shows His unchanging nature, reinforces the unity of Scripture, and deepens our understanding of His work in us now.

Section 4: Key Scriptures

Genesis 1:2

The Spirit is introduced on page one of Scripture—hovering over the waters during creation.

- **The Spirit's Role in Creation** – A powerful force bringing form out of chaos.
- **Ruach as Life and Movement** – The Hebrew word suggests breath, energy, and presence.
- **God's Eternal Presence** – The Spirit wasn't created—He is Creator.

Reflection Questions:

Q1. What does the Spirit's presence in creation tell us about His role in life and order?

Q2. How does this shape your view of the Spirit's power?

Numbers 11:25

The Spirit empowers 70 elders to prophesy alongside Moses.

- **Temporary Empowerment** – The Spirit came upon them for a moment, enabling them to lead and speak.
- **Shared Leadership** – God's Spirit equips not just individuals, but teams.
- **Foreshadowing Pentecost** – This event hints at a day when the Spirit would be poured out on all believers.

Reflection Questions:

Q1. Why was it important for the Spirit to empower these elders temporarily?

Q2. How does this show God's desire to work through His people?

Judges 6:34

The Spirit "clothed" Gideon, giving him the boldness to lead Israel into battle.

- **Divine Empowerment for Leadership** – The Spirit didn't

just assist; He equipped fully.

- **Clothed with Power** – The phrase suggests being wrapped or infused with strength.
- **God Uses the Unlikely** – Gideon was fearful—but the Spirit made him fearless.

Reflection Questions:

Q1. What does it mean to be "clothed" with the Spirit today?

Q2. How does Gideon's story encourage you in moments of doubt?

1 Samuel 16:13-14

The Spirit comes upon David but departs from Saul.

- **Conditional Presence** – In the Old Testament, the Spirit came and went depending on obedience.
- **Empowering a New King** – David's reign began with Spirit-filled authority.
- **A Shadow of the New Covenant** – In Christ, the Spirit remains in us permanently.

Reflection Questions:

Q1. Why did the Spirit leave Saul but remain with David?

Q2. What does this teach us about obedience and God's presence?

Ezekiel 11:5

The Spirit falls upon Ezekiel and enables him to speak God's Word.

- **The Spirit as Messenger** – He empowered prophets to declare God's truth.
- **Divine Authority in Words** – Ezekiel didn't speak his own ideas but was moved by the Spirit.
- **God Still Speaks** – The same Spirit who spoke through Ezekiel guides us today.

Reflection Questions:

Q1. How does this verse show the Spirit's role in revealing truth?

Q2. What does it teach you about listening to the Spirit today?

Section 5: Summary

The Holy Spirit wasn't an afterthought in God's story—He was there from the start. In the Old Testament, He moved powerfully through creation, leadership, and prophecy. While His presence was temporary and selective then, He was preparing the world for something permanent and personal: His indwelling in us today.

Don't overlook the Old Testament. The Spirit you walk with is the same Spirit who gave Samson strength, filled the Tabernacle with glory, and spoke life into Ezekiel's dry bones.

Section 6: Application

- **Reflect on Continuity** – The Spirit hasn't changed; His work continues through you.
- **Pray for Empowerment** – Ask God to clothe you with the same courage He gave Gideon.
- **Study the Prophets** – Look for how the Spirit shaped their lives and words.
- **Live With Confidence** – If the Spirit moved in mighty ways then, expect Him to move in you now.

Daily Practices:

- Begin each morning with this prayer: "Holy Spirit, empower me today like You empowered the leaders of old."
- Meditate on a passage that mentions the Spirit's Old Testament work.
- Journal: Where do you need boldness or wisdom today? Ask

the Spirit to provide it.

Section 7: Reflection Questions

How does seeing the Spirit's work in the Old Testament change your understanding of Him?

In what area of your life do you need the Spirit's empowerment?

How does this lesson deepen your appreciation for the continuity of God's plan?

Section 8: Prayer Prompt (ACTS Model)

Adoration – Holy Spirit, You are eternal. You have moved in power from the beginning. I worship You as the breath of life and the voice of truth.

Confession – Forgive me for ignoring the Old Testament or thinking You were not active until Pentecost.

Thanksgiving – Thank You for empowering flawed people like Gideon and speaking through prophets like Ezekiel. You use the willing—not the perfect.

Supplication – Teach me to recognize Your presence through-out all of Scripture. Empower me today as You did those who walked before me.

Example Prayer:

Holy Spirit, thank You for showing me that You have always been present. Help me to walk in boldness and truth like those You empowered in the past. Give me a heart that listens and a life that responds. Amen.

4

Lesson 3: The Holy Spirit in the Life of Jesus

Key Truth:

Jesus lived a Spirit-empowered life—not to show off His divinity, but to show us how to walk in the Spirit daily.

Section 1: Introduction

Illustration:

Picture a concert pianist performing a masterful composition. Every note flows with precision, not because the pianist is improvising, but because he's in perfect sync with the composer's vision. Jesus' life was like that—every word, every miracle, every step flowed in perfect harmony with the Holy Spirit.

Personal Connection:

Many believers wonder: "If Jesus was God, why did He need the Holy Spirit?" The answer reveals something powerful—not only about Jesus' humility, but also about how *we* are meant to live. Jesus submitted to the Spirit to model the Spirit-led life we're called to walk.

In-Depth Background:

Throughout His life, Jesus was conceived, baptized, led, empowered, and raised by the Holy Spirit. He didn't rely on His divine nature to perform miracles or resist temptation—He relied on the Spirit. This wasn't a concession; it was an example. If Jesus needed the Spirit, how much more do we?

A Personal Example:

I once mentored a young man preparing for ministry who assumed Jesus performed miracles simply because He was divine. When we studied the Gospels together, he stopped me in Luke 4 and said, "Wait... Jesus didn't rely on His own divine power? He depended on the Spirit?" That moment reshaped his whole theology. "So if Jesus needed the Spirit," he said, "then I really can't do this on my own." It shifted his focus from trying to be impressive to learning how to be led.

Section 2: Goals of the Lesson

By the end of this lesson, students will:

1. Understand the Holy Spirit's involvement in every stage of Jesus' life.
2. Learn why Jesus chose to depend on the Spirit.

3. Discover how Jesus models a Spirit-empowered life.
4. Apply the example of Christ to their own walk with the Holy Spirit.

Section 3: Introduction Questions

Why did Jesus, who was fully God, need the Holy Spirit?

Though fully divine, Jesus chose to live as a man submitted to the Spirit to set an example for us.

What does Jesus' dependence on the Spirit teach us?

It shows that the power we need for daily life, ministry, and obedience comes from the Holy Spirit.

How can we follow Jesus' model of Spirit-led living?

By staying connected through prayer, Scripture, obedience, and being sensitive to the Spirit's guidance.

Section 4: Key Scriptures

Luke 1:35

The angel told Mary the Holy Spirit would come upon her, and the power of the Most High would overshadow her—marking Jesus' miraculous conception.

- **Divine Conception** – Jesus' birth was not natural, but supernatural.
- **The Spirit and Incarnation** – From the very beginning, Jesus' humanity was intertwined with the Spirit.
- **God's Glory in Flesh** – The Spirit brought forth the holy Son of God into the world.

Reflection Questions:

Q1. Why was it necessary for Jesus to be conceived by the Spirit?

Q2. What does this tell you about the Spirit's power to create and bring life?

Luke 3:21-22

At Jesus' baptism, the Holy Spirit descended on Him like a dove, and the Father's voice declared, "This is My beloved Son."

- **Trinitarian Moment** – Father, Son, and Spirit all appear together.

- **Anointing for Ministry** – The Spirit marked the beginning of Jesus' public work.
- **Divine Approval** – The Spirit's descent was a visible sign of God's pleasure.

Reflection Questions:

Q1. What does the Spirit's presence at Jesus' baptism say about His mission?

Q2. How can you recognize the Spirit's anointing in your own life?

Luke 4:1,14,18

Jesus, full of the Holy Spirit, was led into the wilderness, and returned in the power of the Spirit to begin His ministry.

- **Spirit-Led Testing** – The Spirit led Jesus into a place of hardship, not comfort.
- **Power to Proclaim** – Jesus' ministry was fueled by Spirit-empowered preaching.
- **The Spirit's Mission** – Jesus declared He was anointed to preach good news, heal the broken, and set captives free.

Reflection Questions:

Q1. Why would the Spirit lead Jesus into the wilderness?

Q2. What does Spirit-empowered ministry look like in your context?

Matthew 12:28

Jesus said, "If I cast out demons by the Spirit of God, then the kingdom of God has come upon you."

- **Miracles by the Spirit** – Jesus didn't use His divine power but relied on the Spirit.
- **Kingdom Authority** – The Spirit brings visible evidence of God's reign.
- **Accessible Power** – The same Spirit that empowered Jesus empowers us.

Reflection Questions:

Q1. How does Jesus' reliance on the Spirit challenge your view of miracles?

Q2. What confidence does this give you in facing spiritual battles?

Romans 8:11

The same Spirit who raised Jesus from the dead lives in you.

- **Resurrection Power** – The Spirit didn't just sustain Jesus in life—He raised Him from death.
- **Indwelling Spirit** – That same resurrection power now resides in believers.
- **Hope and Strength** – You have the power of life living inside you.

Reflection Questions:

Q1. What does it mean to live with resurrection power?

Q2. How can this verse shape your expectations of the Spirit's role in your life?

Section 5: Summary

The Holy Spirit was present at every step of Jesus' earthly life— from conception to resurrection. Jesus didn't lean on His divine identity to perform miracles, overcome temptation, or teach with authority. He relied fully on the Spirit to empower Him for everything He did.

This wasn't weakness—it was obedience. Jesus submitted to the Spirit's leading so we could follow His example. If Jesus depended on the Spirit, we must do the same.

If the Son of God needed the Spirit, so do you. Don't live in

your own strength—live empowered.

Section 6: Application

- **Follow Jesus' Example** – Choose dependence over self-sufficiency.
- **Invite the Spirit Daily** – Begin your day by acknowledging His presence.
- **Step Out in Faith** – Just as Jesus proclaimed His mission in Luke 4:18, boldly embrace your Spirit-given calling.

Daily Practices:

- Begin each day with this prayer: "Holy Spirit, lead me today like You led Jesus."
- Meditate on Luke 4:18 and ask the Spirit to empower you to live it out.
- Journal: Where in your life are you trying to operate without the Spirit?

Section 7: Reflection Questions

What does Jesus' dependence on the Spirit teach you about your own walk with God?

In what areas of your life are you relying on your own strength?

How can you begin living more like Jesus—led and empowered by the Holy Spirit?

Section 8: Prayer Prompt (ACTS Model)

Adoration – Holy Spirit, I praise You for empowering Jesus and for living in me. You are the power of God, the giver of life, and the voice of truth.

Confession – Forgive me for trying to follow Jesus without depending on the Spirit like He did.

Thanksgiving – Thank You for being the same Spirit who raised Jesus from the dead and now dwells in me.

Supplication – Help me walk in the power of the Spirit, speak with boldness, and love with compassion like Jesus did.

Example Prayer:

Holy Spirit, thank You for empowering Jesus in every moment of His earthly life. I confess that I often try to live in my own strength. Teach me to rely on You as Jesus did. Fill me with courage, truth, and purpose. May my life reflect the One who lives in me. Amen.

5

Lesson 4: The Role of the Holy Spirit in Salvation

Key Truth:

Salvation is not just a moment of belief—it's a miracle of transformation made possible by the Holy Spirit.

Section 1: Introduction

Illustration:

Imagine a ship lost at sea in complete darkness. The sailors on board cannot see the way forward and are drifting aimlessly. Suddenly, a lighthouse appears in the distance, shining a guiding light that leads them safely to shore. The Holy Spirit is like that lighthouse—illuminating the path to salvation, convicting hearts, and guiding us toward faith in Jesus Christ.

Personal Connection:

Many people think salvation begins with a decision they make. But Scripture reveals a deeper truth: salvation begins with the Spirit drawing us, convicting us, and regenerating our hearts. We don't find God—He finds us. This lesson will uncover the Spirit's essential role in your salvation story.

In-Depth Background:

The Greek word for Spirit, *pneuma*, means breath or wind, signifying life and movement. Just as physical life requires breath, spiritual life requires the regenerating work of the Holy Spirit. He convicts, regenerates, seals, and assures—doing the work we could never do ourselves.

A Personal Example:

I'll never forget the night a teenager in our youth group came forward in tears after hearing about the Spirit's role in salvation. She'd grown up thinking being saved meant trying really hard to be good. But when she heard that the Spirit convicts, regenerates, and seals us—without us earning it— she whispered, "So I don't have to fake it anymore?" That night she stopped striving and simply trusted. Her transformation wasn't flashy, but it was deep—and her confidence grew from knowing it wasn't about her grip on God, but His grip on her.

Section 2: Goals of the Lesson

By the end of this lesson, students will:

1. Understand the Holy Spirit's role in conviction, regenera-

tion, adoption, sealing, and assurance.
2. Recognize that salvation is a work of God, not human effort.
3. Find confidence in the Spirit's sealing and assurance.
4. Learn how the Spirit's work in salvation fuels evangelism.

Section 3: Introduction Questions

How does a person come to faith in Christ?

Not simply by choice, but by the Spirit's conviction and drawing (John 6:44).

What does it mean to be "born again" by the Spirit?

It means receiving new spiritual life through the Spirit's regeneration.

Can a believer lose their salvation?

No. The Spirit seals and secures our salvation until the day of redemption.

Section 4: Key Scriptures

John 16:8-11

The Spirit convicts the world of sin, righteousness, and judgment.

- **Conviction of Sin** – The Spirit reveals humanity's sin and our need for a Savior.
- **Conviction of Righteousness** – He shows us that true righteousness is found in Christ.
- **Conviction of Judgment** – He warns that sin has consequences and Christ has overcome.

Reflection Questions:

Q1. Why is conviction necessary before someone can be saved?

Q2. Have you ever experienced the Spirit's conviction personally? What did it lead to?

John 3:5-6

Jesus said, "Unless one is born of water and the Spirit, he cannot enter the kingdom of God."

- **Born of the Spirit** – Salvation requires spiritual rebirth, not just religious action.
- **Cleansing and Renewal** – Symbolized by water, fulfilled by

the Spirit.
- **Flesh vs. Spirit** – Human birth brings physical life; only the Spirit gives eternal life.

Reflection Questions:

Q1. What does it mean to be born again by the Spirit?

Q2. How does this new birth change a person's desires and direction?

Titus 3:5
"He saved us... by the washing of regeneration and renewal of the Holy Spirit."

- **Regeneration** – A total rebirth—new identity, new heart, new purpose.
- **By His Mercy** – Salvation is not earned, but received through God's grace.
- **Ongoing Renewal** – The Spirit continues to shape us daily into Christ's image.

Reflection Questions:

Q1. Why is salvation based on God's mercy, not human effort?

Q2. How is the Spirit renewing you right now?

Romans 8:15-16

"You have received the Spirit of adoption... the Spirit bears witness that we are God's children."

- **Adopted by God** – The Spirit brings us into a personal, intimate relationship with the Father.
- **Abba, Father** – We approach God not in fear, but in love.
- **Assurance of Identity** – The Spirit reminds us we belong to God.

Reflection Questions:

Q1. How does adoption shape your view of your relationship with God?

Q2. What comfort does the Spirit's witness bring to your faith?

Ephesians 1:13-14

"You were sealed with the Holy Spirit... the guarantee of our inheritance."

- **Sealed by the Spirit** – A permanent mark of ownership and protection.

- **Guarantee of What's to Come** – The Spirit is a down payment on eternal life.
- **Security in Christ** – Our salvation is not fragile—it's secured by God.

Reflection Questions:

Q1. How does being sealed by the Spirit give you confidence in your salvation?

Q2. How does this promise affect your day-to-day spiritual life?

Section 5: Summary

The Holy Spirit is not only present at the moment of salvation— He makes it possible. From conviction to regeneration, from adoption to sealing, the Spirit is behind every part of our spiritual rebirth. Salvation is not a one-time decision made in our strength, but a divine miracle initiated and sustained by the Spirit of God.

If you're saved, it's because the Spirit opened your eyes, changed your heart, and gave you new life. That same Spirit now lives in you and guarantees your future.

41

Section 6: Application

- **Reflect on your salvation story** – Where can you now see the Spirit's fingerprints?
- **Thank God for the Spirit's work** – Worship isn't just for Jesus—it's for the Spirit too.
- **Share your testimony** – Let others know how the Spirit drew you to Christ.

Daily Practices:

- Each morning, thank the Holy Spirit for saving and sealing you.
- Write down 3 ways your life has changed since being born again.
- Pray specifically for someone who needs conviction and salvation.

Section 7: Reflection Questions

How has the Holy Spirit worked in your life to bring about salvation?

What does it mean to be sealed and secured by the Spirit?

Who can you begin praying for that the Spirit would convict and draw to Christ?

Section 8: Prayer Prompt (ACTS Model)

Adoration – Holy Spirit, You are the One who gives life, opens blind eyes, and brings hearts to Jesus. I praise You for being my Guide, Convictor, and Comforter.

Confession – Forgive me for taking my salvation for granted, for forgetting the miracle You've worked in me.

Thanksgiving – Thank You for convicting my heart, regenerating my spirit, adopting me into God's family, and sealing me forever.

Supplication – Stir my heart for the lost. Use me as a vessel of Your grace. Empower my words and prayers so others might know Your saving power.

Example Prayer:

Holy Spirit, I am saved because You called me, convicted me, and gave me life. Thank You for sealing me with Your presence and for reminding me daily that I am a child of God. Help me walk with gratitude, live with confidence, and speak boldly so others might know You too. Amen.

6

Lesson 5: The Indwelling of the Holy Spirit

Key Truth:

The Spirit doesn't just visit—you are His home.

Section 1: Introduction

Illustration:

Imagine receiving a priceless gift—a personal guide who knows every challenge you will face and offers wisdom, strength, and comfort at every turn. This guide doesn't come and go—he stays. He's always present, always ready to lead and help. The Holy Spirit is that guide. From the moment of salvation, He moves in and never moves out.

Personal Connection:

Many Christians live as if they're alone—navigating life without the awareness of the Spirit's presence. But Scripture teaches that the Holy Spirit makes His home in every believer. He's not an occasional visitor or a spiritual upgrade. He is God dwelling within you.

In-Depth Background:

The Greek word for dwelling, *oikeō*, means to make a home, to reside permanently. This is not a symbolic idea. It's a spiritual reality. Unlike the Old Testament, where the Spirit came upon people temporarily, the New Testament reveals that every believer is indwelt permanently by the Holy Spirit. This changes everything.

A Personal Example:

A woman in our small group once confessed, "I always felt like I had to 'feel' the Holy Spirit for Him to be with me." She feared that when she messed up, He would leave. As we walked through Ephesians 1 and John 14 together, her eyes welled up. "You mean... He actually lives in me? Always?" That truth didn't just change how she thought—it gave her peace. She started praying differently, walking more confidently, and stopped believing every spiritual dry spell meant God had left her.

Section 2: Goals of the Lesson

By the end of this lesson, students will:

1. Understand the permanence of the Holy Spirit's in-

dwelling.
2. Recognize the transformative impact of His presence.
3. Find assurance in the Spirit's unbreakable seal.
4. Learn to live daily with Spirit-awareness.

Section 3: Introduction Questions

What does it mean for the Holy Spirit to dwell in you?

It means God Himself takes up residence in your life, guiding, convicting, and empowering you from within.

Can the Holy Spirit leave a believer?

No. Unlike the temporary presence in the Old Testament, the Spirit's indwelling is permanent (Ephesians 1:13-14).

How should knowing the Spirit lives in you change your daily mindset?

It brings confidence, conviction, and a deep sense of belonging to God.

Section 4: Key Scriptures

John 14:16-17

Jesus promises the Spirit will be with believers forever.

- **Permanent Helper** – The Spirit is not a visitor but a lifelong companion.
- **The Spirit of Truth** – He teaches, reminds, and clarifies God's truth.
- **You Know Him** – He lives with you and will be in you— personally.

Reflection Questions:

Q1. Why is permanence such a powerful promise?

Q2. How do you personally experience the Spirit's guidance?

Romans 8:9-11

Paul teaches that the Spirit of God dwells in every true believer.

- **The Spirit Marks Belonging** – If you don't have the Spirit, you don't belong to Christ.
- **Power for Life** – The Spirit gives life to our mortal bodies.
- **Indwelling Assurance** – The same Spirit that raised Jesus now empowers you.

Reflection Questions:

Q1. What does it mean to be defined by the Spirit's presence?

Q2. How does this truth affect your battle with sin or discouragement?

1 Corinthians 6:19-20

Your body is a temple of the Holy Spirit.

- **God Lives in You** – No longer in tents or temples—the Spirit now resides in believers.
- **You Are Not Your Own** – You were bought with a price, and you carry God's presence.
- **Call to Holiness** – Your choices reflect the indwelling reality.

Reflection Questions:

Q1. What does treating your body as God's temple look like practically?

Q2. How does this verse raise the bar for your daily choices?

Ephesians 1:13-14

The Spirit is a seal and a guarantee of our inheritance.

- **Ownership and Security** – The Spirit is God's "stamp" confirming you are His.
- **Guaranteed Future** – Eternal life is not uncertain—it's guaranteed.
- **Confidence to Live Boldly** – You're sealed. You're His. Act like it.

Reflection Questions:

Q1. What fears does the Spirit's seal eliminate in your life?

Q2. How should this security fuel your spiritual growth?

Section 5: Summary

The indwelling of the Holy Spirit is not a symbolic metaphor. It is a spiritual reality. You don't have to chase God's presence—you carry it. The Spirit's indwelling brings power for living, assurance in salvation, and constant access to divine guidance.

You are a living temple. The Holy Spirit resides in you—

49

not temporarily, not occasionally, but forever. Live with that awareness.

Section 6: Application

- **Practice Spirit-Awareness** – Pause throughout the day to acknowledge His presence.
- **Honor the Temple** – Let your habits, words, and attitudes reflect His holiness.
- **Rest in Assurance** – You are sealed. Live with confidence, not fear.

Daily Practices:

- Begin your morning with this prayer: "Holy Spirit, thank You for dwelling in me. Lead me today."
- Set an hourly reminder on your phone to pause and acknowledge His presence.
- Journal at night: Where did you sense the Spirit today?

Section 7: Reflection Questions

How does knowing the Spirit lives in you change your perspective?

What area of your life needs to reflect His holiness more clearly?

In what ways can you grow in daily awareness of His presence?

Section 8: Prayer Prompt (ACTS Model)

Adoration – Holy Spirit, I praise You for choosing to dwell in me. You are not distant, but near. You are God in me.

Confession – Forgive me for ignoring Your presence or treating my life as if I'm alone.

Thanksgiving – Thank You for sealing me, leading me, and empowering me. I am never alone.

Supplication – Make me more aware of Your indwelling presence. Help me live in a way that honors You as Your temple.

Example Prayer:

Holy Spirit, thank You for living in me. Help me walk in a way that reflects Your presence. Make me sensitive to Your guidance, quick to respond to conviction, and bold to live as Your dwelling place. Remind me today that I carry Your power and peace wherever I go. Amen.

7

Lesson 6: The Baptism of the Holy Spirit

Key Truth:

The baptism of the Holy Spirit is the moment God places you into His family and empowers you to live for His mission.

Section 1: Introduction

Illustration:

   Imagine a dry sponge placed into a bowl of water. The moment it touches the water, it's completely immersed and saturated. The water fills every part of the sponge, changing its texture and making it useful. That's what happens at the baptism of the Holy Spirit—we are fully immersed into the life of Christ and the community of believers, made useful for His purpose.

Personal Connection:

There's a lot of confusion around Spirit baptism. Some think it's an emotional second experience after salvation. Others think it's the same as being filled with the Spirit. But the Bible offers clarity—Spirit baptism happens at salvation and places you into the body of Christ. This lesson will help you separate myth from truth and embrace what God has already done in you.

In-Depth Background:

The Greek word *baptizō* means to immerse or submerge. All four Gospels and the book of Acts refer to Spirit baptism, showing its significance in the life of the believer. It is not about feelings, but about **identity and empowerment**. When you're baptized by the Holy Spirit, you are placed in Christ, sealed with the Spirit, and called into mission.

A Personal Example:

A young man once approached me after a message and asked, "Do I need a second baptism to really experience the Holy Spirit?" He had heard different teachings that made him feel spiritually "less than" because he hadn't spoken in tongues or had some emotional experience. We opened 1 Corinthians 12:13 together and read about how every believer is baptized into one body by the Spirit. He exhaled deeply. "So I've had the Spirit all along?" he asked. That understanding lifted a burden of striving and comparison—and replaced it with gratitude and confidence in what God had already done.

Section 2: Goals of the Lesson

By the end of this lesson, students will:

1. Understand the biblical meaning of the baptism of the Holy Spirit.
2. Distinguish between Spirit baptism, indwelling, and filling.
3. Recognize that Spirit baptism happens once—at salvation.
4. Embrace the Spirit's empowerment for living and serving.

Section 3: Introduction Questions

What is the baptism of the Holy Spirit, and when does it happen?

It's when the Spirit immerses you into Christ's body at the moment of salvation (1 Corinthians 12:13).

How is it different from being filled with the Spirit?

Baptism happens once at salvation. Filling happens repeatedly and empowers daily living.

Why does understanding Spirit baptism matter?

It gives you confidence in your salvation, assurance of your identity, and power for your purpose.

Section 4: Key Scriptures

Matthew 3:11

John the Baptist points to Jesus as the One who will baptize with the Holy Spirit and fire.

- **New Covenant Promise** – Jesus doesn't just forgive sin—He immerses believers in power.
- **Spirit and Fire** – The Spirit purifies, refines, and empowers.
- **Christ as the Baptizer** – Baptism in the Spirit comes through Jesus, not man.

Reflection Questions:

Q1. Why is it important that Jesus is the one who baptizes with the Holy Spirit?

Q2. What does the imagery of fire teach us about the Spirit's role in your life?

Acts 1:4-5, 8

Jesus promises His disciples they will be baptized with the Spirit and empowered for mission.

- **Promise Fulfilled** – What John prophesied, Jesus confirms.
- **Power for Purpose** – The baptism equips for witness, not for private experience.
- **Global Mission** – Spirit baptism connects us to God's plan to reach the world.

Reflection Questions:

Q1. What connection do you see between Spirit baptism and being a witness?

Q2. How has the Spirit empowered you for mission?

Acts 2:1-4

The day of Pentecost marks the fulfillment of the promise, as the Spirit is poured out.

- **The Spirit Comes** – Not on one person, but on all who believe.
- **Unity and Boldness** – The baptism creates a community and a message.
- **Birth of the Church** – This is the moment the Church goes public in power.

Reflection Questions:

Q1. How does this moment compare to your view of the Church?

Q2. What does this teach us about the communal nature of Spirit baptism?

1 Corinthians 12:13

Paul affirms that all believers are baptized by one Spirit into one body.

- **Universal Experience** – Every believer is baptized in the Spirit.
- **Spiritual Unity** – No believer is excluded or second-class.
- **Into One Body** – Spirit baptism connects us to Christ and to each other.

Reflection Questions:

Q1. How does this verse debunk the idea that Spirit baptism is only for some?

Q2. What does it mean for you to be "part of one body" through the Spirit?

Ephesians 4:5

Paul says there is one Lord, one faith, one baptism.

- **Oneness of Faith** – The Spirit unites all believers.

- **Singular Baptism** – It happens once—at salvation—not as a later event.
- **Unified Identity** – You are part of something bigger than yourself.

Reflection Questions:

Q1. How does this truth bring clarity to confusion around Spirit baptism?

Q2. Why is spiritual unity so important in the life of the Church?

Section 5: Summary

The baptism of the Holy Spirit is not an emotional high—it's a spiritual reality. It happens once, at salvation, when you are placed into the body of Christ. You are immersed into Jesus, sealed by the Spirit, and empowered for God's mission.

You don't need to chase another experience—you need to walk in what God has already done.

Section 6: Application

- **Rest in the Reality** – If you are in Christ, you've been baptized by the Spirit.
- **Live from Your Identity** – You are part of God's family and mission.
- **Seek the Filling Daily** – Baptism happens once. Filling happens often. Stay surrendered.

Daily Practices:

- Declare aloud: "I am baptized by the Spirit into the body of Christ."
- Pray for boldness to be a witness wherever you go.
- Look for opportunities to serve the body of Christ you've been baptized into.

Section 7: Reflection Questions

How does understanding Spirit baptism change your view of your salvation?

What role does Spirit baptism play in your mission and calling?

In what ways can you live more aware of your place in the body of Christ?

How does this teaching reshape how you view your relationship with other believers?

Section 8: Prayer Prompt (ACTS Model)

Adoration – Holy Spirit, You are the One who places me in Christ and empowers me for His mission. I praise You for Your perfect work in salvation and purpose.

Confession – Forgive me for misunderstanding or minimizing the power of Spirit baptism. Forgive me for trying to live out my faith without Your leading.

Thanksgiving – Thank You for immersing me into the body of Christ. Thank You for the unity, power, and purpose that comes through Your baptism.

Supplication – Help me walk in the reality of my baptism daily. Fill me afresh. Empower me to live boldly, serve faithfully, and love deeply as part of Your Church.

Example Prayer:

Holy Spirit, thank You for baptizing me into the body of Christ. Thank You that I am not alone—that I belong, that I'm empowered, and that I'm called. Help me live like it. Lead me to walk in the power You provide and fulfill the mission You've given. Amen.

8

Lesson 7: The Fruit of the Holy Spirit

Key Truth:

Spiritual fruit isn't achieved through effort—it's grown through surrender.

Section 1: Introduction

Illustration:

Imagine a tree planted beside a steady stream, its roots sinking deep into nourishing soil. Over time, it grows strong and produces abundant fruit—not because it tries harder, but because it stays connected to its source. The Christian life is no different. When we walk with the Spirit, we bear fruit that reflects the character of Christ.

Personal Connection:

Many believers strive to be more loving, patient, or kind—but striving isn't the answer. The fruit of the Spirit isn't something we manufacture. It's something the Spirit grows in us as we remain connected to Christ. This lesson will help you understand what the fruit is, how it grows, and how you can cultivate a life that produces lasting spiritual fruit.

In-Depth Background:

Galatians 5:22–23 lists the fruit of the Spirit—not as nine separate fruits, but as one collective result of the Spirit's presence in a believer. These characteristics reflect the heart of Jesus and reveal spiritual maturity. While spiritual gifts differ among believers, the fruit of the Spirit is meant to be present in every Christian's life.

A Personal Example:

I once met a man who said, "I've tried for years to be more patient, and it just makes me more frustrated." He treated the fruit of the Spirit like a self-improvement checklist. But when he started spending regular time in prayer and Scripture—not to perform, but to connect with the Spirit—his wife noticed the difference first. "You're calmer lately," she said. "More joyful." He hadn't even realized the shift. That's when it clicked: it wasn't about forcing fruit. It was about staying connected to the source.

Section 2: Goals of the Lesson

By the end of this lesson, students will:

1. Understand that the fruit of the Spirit is the evidence of a Spirit-led life.
2. Recognize the contrast between the works of the flesh and the fruit of the Spirit.
3. Learn how spiritual fruit is cultivated, not forced.
4. Identify areas where they can yield more fully to the Spirit's work.

Section 3: Introduction Questions

What is the fruit of the Spirit?

It's the natural result of a life surrendered to the Holy Spirit—character traits that reflect Christ.

Why does Paul call it "fruit" and not "fruits"?

Because it's one cohesive work of the Spirit, not a menu of options. These qualities grow together, not in isolation.

How do we cultivate the fruit of the Spirit?

By abiding in Christ and walking with the Spirit daily.

Section 4: Key Scriptures

Galatians 5:22–23

Paul contrasts the works of the flesh with the fruit of the Spirit.

- **Spirit-Produced Character** – Love, joy, peace, patience, kindness, goodness, faithfulness, gentleness, and self-control.
- **Evidence of Surrender** – The fruit reveals who is truly walking with God.
- **No Law Against It** – This fruit naturally fulfills God's will.

Reflection Questions:

Q1. Why is it significant that these traits are called "fruit" instead of "works"?

Q2. Which aspects of the fruit do you feel are flourishing—or struggling—in your life?

John 15:4–5

Jesus teaches that abiding in Him produces fruit.

- **Abide to Bear** – Fruit is the result of remaining connected to Jesus.

- **Apart From Me** – We cannot produce godly character on our own.
- **Spiritual Vitality** – Fruitfulness flows from intimacy with Christ.

Reflection Questions:

Q1. What does it look like to abide in Christ daily?

Q2. How can you remain more rooted in Him this week?

Matthew 7:16–20

Jesus says we recognize people by their fruit.

- **Fruit Reveals Identity** – What we produce shows who we truly are.
- **False Teachers Lack Fruit** – Sound teaching and godly character go hand-in-hand.
- **Spiritual Discernment** – We are called to inspect—not judge—by fruit.

Reflection Questions:

Q1. How does this challenge your understanding of spiritual maturity?

Q2. What does your current fruit say about your walk with God?

Section 5: Summary

The fruit of the Spirit is not something we strive for—it's something we surrender to. When we stay connected to Christ and walk in the Spirit, our lives naturally begin to reflect His character. Love, joy, peace, and all the other qualities listed are not checkboxes to complete—they are outcomes of transformation.

Don't focus on producing fruit. Focus on abiding. The Spirit will handle the growth.

Section 6: Application

- **Check the Soil** – Are you staying rooted in Christ through prayer, Word, and worship?
- **Let the Spirit Prune You** – Be willing to let go of habits and attitudes that block growth.
- **Celebrate Growth** – Look for ways God is already producing fruit in you.

Daily Practices:

- Reflect on one fruit of the Spirit each day. Ask God to grow that quality in you.

- Memorize Galatians 5:22–23 and meditate on it throughout the week.
- Ask a trusted friend or mentor: "Where do you see the Spirit's fruit in me? Where can I grow?"

Section 7: Reflection Questions

Which fruit of the Spirit stands out as an area where you need growth?

What's one practical step you can take to abide more deeply in Christ?

How can you create space in your life for the Spirit to produce fruit?

Section 8: Prayer Prompt (ACTS Model)

Adoration – Holy Spirit, You are the source of true growth and godly character. I worship You as the one who transforms my heart from the inside out.

Confession – Forgive me for trying to bear fruit in my own strength—or for settling for spiritual stagnation.

Thanksgiving – Thank You for Your patience and power in growing love, joy, peace, and more within me.

Supplication – Help me stay connected to You, rooted in Christ, and open to correction. Produce lasting fruit in me that reflects Your nature.

Example Prayer:

Holy Spirit, I don't want to fake fruit—I want the real thing. Help me abide in Christ and walk in step with You. Cultivate love where there is selfishness, peace where there is stress, and joy where there is discouragement. Make me more like Jesus each day. Amen.

9

Lesson 8: The Role of the Holy Spirit in Sanctification

Key Truth:

Sanctification is not about trying harder—it's about surrendering deeper to the Spirit's transforming work.

Section 1: Introduction

Illustration:

Picture a sculptor carefully shaping a block of marble. With every deliberate strike of the chisel, he removes what doesn't belong—bit by bit revealing the masterpiece within. That's how the Holy Spirit works in us. He patiently chips away at everything that doesn't look like Jesus, shaping us into His image.

Personal Connection:

Many believers feel like failures in their spiritual growth because they think it's all up to them. But sanctification—the process of becoming more like Christ—is not fueled by self-discipline alone. It's the ongoing work of the Holy Spirit in you. When you understand His role, you'll stop striving and start yielding.

In-Depth Background:

Sanctification means "to be set apart." In Scripture, it has both a positional and progressive meaning. Positionally, we are sanctified in Christ the moment we are saved. Progressively, we grow in holiness through the Spirit's work over time. He convicts, guides, teaches, and transforms us through trials, truth, and obedience. It's not about perfection—it's about progress, powered by the Spirit.

A Personal Example:

A friend of mine once told me, "I thought sanctification meant I had to clean myself up so God would be proud of me." He kept falling into the same sin, then beating himself up, thinking he had to try harder. But one night he came across 2 Corinthians 3:18 and realized the Spirit was the One doing the transforming—not him alone. That shift didn't make him passive. It made him more surrendered. He stopped striving to impress God and started inviting the Spirit to change him from the inside out—and over time, the change came.

Section 2: Goals of the Lesson

By the end of this lesson, students will:

1. Understand the difference between justification and sanctification.
2. Learn how the Holy Spirit actively sanctifies believers over time.
3. Identify their role in cooperating with the Spirit through spiritual disciplines.
4. Commit to surrendering daily to the Spirit's refining work.

Section 3: Introduction Questions

What is sanctification, and how is it different from justification?

Justification happens once—we are declared righteous. Sanctification is the ongoing process of being made righteous.

How does the Holy Spirit participate in sanctification?

He convicts us of sin, renews our minds, produces fruit, and empowers us to obey.

Is sanctification automatic or does it require effort?

It's a partnership. The Spirit works in us, but we must yield and participate through obedience and discipline.

Section 4: Key Scriptures

John 17:17

Jesus prayed, "Sanctify them by Your truth. Your word is truth."

- **Truth Transforms** – The Spirit uses Scripture to refine and guide us.
- **Set Apart for Purpose** – Sanctification prepares us for God's use.
- **Jesus' Prayer for Us** – He desires our growth in holiness.

Reflection Questions:

Q1. How are you allowing God's truth to shape you right now?

Q2. What does this verse say about the connection between God's Word and sanctification?

Romans 8:13–14

Paul writes that by the Spirit, we put to death the deeds of the body.

- **Spirit-Empowered Obedience** – Victory over sin is possible through the Spirit.
- **Ongoing Battle** – Sanctification is daily warfare.
- **Led by the Spirit** – He leads us into righteousness, not just out of sin.

Reflection Questions:

Q1. What areas of your life is the Spirit convicting you to surrender?

Q2. How do you fight sin with the Spirit's help instead of your own strength?

2 Corinthians 3:18

We are being transformed into Christ's image from glory to glory.

- **Gradual Change** – Sanctification takes time.
- **Spirit-Driven Process** – Transformation is not self-powered.
- **Reflecting Christ** – The goal is not self-improvement, but Christlikeness.

Reflection Questions:

Q1. Where have you seen the Spirit change you over time?

Q2. How can you cooperate with Him in the areas still under construction?

Galatians 5:16–17

Walk by the Spirit and you won't gratify the flesh.

- **Daily Walking** – Sanctification is a lifestyle, not an event.
- **Tension Between Natures** – The flesh and Spirit are in conflict.
- **Victory in Surrender** – Walking by the Spirit brings freedom.

Reflection Questions:

Q1. What helps you stay in step with the Spirit each day?

Q2. How does walking by the Spirit lead to transformation?

Section 5: Summary

Sanctification is the lifelong work of the Holy Spirit shaping us into the likeness of Christ. It's not about religious performance or perfection—but about daily yielding to the Spirit's refining touch. He uses the Word, relationships, circumstances, and conviction to reveal what needs to go—and to grow.

You don't have to be perfect. You just have to be pliable. Let the Spirit do His work.

Section 6: Application

- **Embrace the Process** – Don't despise small steps of growth.
- **Stay in the Word** – Let Scripture be the chisel God uses to shape you.
- **Invite Conviction** – Ask the Spirit to show you what needs transformation.

Daily Practices:

- Begin your day with this prayer: "Holy Spirit, sanctify me today. Make me more like Jesus."
- Meditate on one fruit of the Spirit and ask how it needs to grow in you.
- Journal: What is God currently refining in your heart and mind?

Section 7: Reflection Questions

What does sanctification currently look like in your life?

How have you resisted or embraced the Spirit's refining work?

What's one habit or mindset you need to surrender to grow?

Section 8: Prayer Prompt (ACTS Model)

Adoration – Holy Spirit, You are the refiner and transformer. I praise You for shaping me into Christ's image.

Confession – Forgive me for resisting Your work or believing I must grow on my own.

Thanksgiving – Thank You for being patient and persistent. Thank You for every step of growth.

Supplication – Continue to sanctify me. Shape my heart, renew my mind, and transform my actions.

Example Prayer:

Holy Spirit, I surrender to Your refining work. I know I can't make myself holy, but You can. Reveal what needs to change and give me the strength to obey. Thank You for not giving up on me. Make me more like Jesus day by day. Amen.

10

Lesson 9: The Holy Spirit in Prayer

Key Truth:

The Holy Spirit turns prayer from duty to dialogue— empowering us to speak, listen, and align with God's heart.

Section 1: Introduction

Illustration:

Imagine a child learning to speak. Their words are simple, broken, sometimes unintelligible. But the parent leans in, understands the heart behind the struggle, and lovingly helps the child express what they feel. That's what the Holy Spirit does for us in prayer—interpreting our groans, guiding our words, and connecting us deeply with the Father.

Personal Connection:

Prayer can feel confusing, repetitive, or even intimidating. But it doesn't have to be. You don't pray alone—the Holy Spirit is your intercessor, teacher, and helper. He lifts your prayers when you don't have the words and helps you pray in alignment with God's will. This lesson will deepen your confidence and freedom in Spirit-led prayer.

In-Depth Background:

The Spirit's role in prayer is central to the believer's spiritual life. Romans 8 teaches that He intercedes when we are weak. Ephesians encourages us to pray in the Spirit at all times. And Jesus Himself promised the Spirit would teach us to pray. Prayer is not a monologue—it's a relationship powered by the Spirit of God.

A Personal Example:

A woman in our church once shared how, after losing her husband, she could barely pray. "I had no words," she said. "Just tears." For weeks, she felt spiritually broken. Then one day while reading Romans 8:26, she wept—not out of grief, but relief. "The Spirit was praying for me," she whispered. "Even when I was silent, God wasn't." That truth didn't take away the pain, but it gave her peace. Her prayer life wasn't restored with eloquence—it was restored with honesty, knowing she never prays alone.

Section 2: Goals of the Lesson

By the end of this lesson, students will:

1. Understand the Holy Spirit's role in guiding, strengthening, and interceding in prayer.
2. Recognize the difference between praying in the flesh and praying in the Spirit.
3. Grow in confidence that their prayers are heard and helped by the Spirit.
4. Learn to develop a Spirit-led rhythm of prayer.

Section 3: Introduction Questions

Why do so many believers struggle with prayer?

Many feel inadequate, distracted, or unsure of what to say. The Spirit helps overcome those barriers.

What does it mean to pray in the Spirit?

It means yielding to the Spirit's guidance—praying in alignment with God's heart, not just our own.

How can the Holy Spirit deepen your prayer life?

By interceding when words fail, guiding your thoughts, and aligning your desires with God's will.

Section 4: Key Scriptures

Romans 8:26–27

The Spirit helps in our weakness and intercedes for us.

- **Our Advocate in Prayer** – The Spirit prays when we can't.
- **Groanings Too Deep** – Even unspoken prayers are heard.
- **Aligned With God's Will** – He ensures our prayers are God-directed.

Reflection Questions:

Q1. When have you felt weak or speechless in prayer?

Q2. How does knowing the Spirit intercedes for you bring comfort?

Ephesians 6:18

Pray in the Spirit on all occasions.

- **Spirit-Led Battle** – Prayer is part of spiritual warfare.
- **Diverse Expressions** – Includes praise, confession, intercession, and more.

- **Perseverance and Watchfulness** – The Spirit sustains us in persistent prayer.

Reflection Questions:

Q1. What does it look like to pray in the Spirit throughout your day?

Q2. How has Spirit-led prayer helped you endure challenges?

Jude 1:20
Build yourselves up in faith and pray in the Holy Spirit.

- **Spiritual Strengthening** – Prayer builds your faith muscles.
- **Spirit-Directed Growth** – You grow by praying as the Spirit leads.
- **Protection from Deception** – Spirit-led prayer anchors you in truth.

Reflection Questions:

Q1. How does prayer increase your spiritual resilience?

Q2. What's one way to begin praying more consistently in the Spirit?

Zechariah 12:10

God promises to pour out a spirit of grace and supplication.

- **Prayer Is a Gift** – Even our desire to pray comes from the Spirit.
- **Spirit-Stirred Intercession** – He burdens our hearts for what burdens God.
- **Grace-Fueled Communication** – The Spirit draws us into God's presence.

Reflection Questions:

Q1. How does the Spirit stir your heart to pray for others?

Q2. What difference does it make to know that prayer begins with grace?

Section 5: Summary

Prayer isn't something you master—it's a relationship you grow into. And you don't grow into it alone. The Holy Spirit strengthens you in weakness, intercedes when you can't speak, and aligns your heart with God's will. He is your helper, your translator, and your prayer partner.

You don't have to pray perfectly. You just have to pray

dependently. The Spirit will do the rest.

Section 6: Application

- **Invite the Spirit Before You Pray** – Ask Him to lead your thoughts and words.
- **Use Scripture** – Let the Spirit guide your prayer through God's Word.
- **Listen More** – Make time to hear what the Spirit impresses on your heart.

Daily Practices:

- Begin each prayer with: "Holy Spirit, lead my words."
- Keep a prayer journal to record what the Spirit brings to mind.
- Pray for someone the Spirit places on your heart—even unexpectedly.

Section 7: Reflection Questions

How does the Spirit change the way you approach prayer?

What distractions or fears can you surrender to pray more freely?

How can you become more attentive to the Spirit's prompting in prayer?

Section 8: Prayer Prompt (ACTS Model)

Adoration – Holy Spirit, I praise You as my helper and intercessor. You know my heart and lead me into deeper intimacy with God.

Confession – Forgive me for treating prayer like a duty or for trying to do it in my own strength.

Thanksgiving – Thank You for helping me when I can't find the words. Thank You for aligning my prayers with God's will.

Supplication – Teach me to listen, to speak, and to trust You in every moment of prayer.

Example Prayer:

Holy Spirit, I invite You into my prayer life. Help me speak what matters and listen to what You are saying. Teach me to rest in Your presence, intercede through me, and align my heart with God's. Even when I don't have the words—You do. Thank You. Amen.

11

Lesson 10: The Gifts of the Holy Spirit

Key Truth:

Spiritual gifts aren't for showing off—they're for building up the body of Christ.

Section 1: Introduction

Illustration:

Imagine a body where the hands refuse to work, the eyes won't open, and the feet refuse to walk. The body exists—but it can't function. That's what the Church looks like when believers ignore or neglect their spiritual gifts. The Holy Spirit gives every believer gifts—not for personal glory, but to serve, encourage, and grow the Church.

Personal Connection:

You have been gifted by the Holy Spirit. Whether you feel equipped or not, the Spirit has placed gifts in you for a reason. Discovering and using your gifts isn't about being super-spiritual—it's about being available. This lesson will help you understand what spiritual gifts are, why they matter, and how you can use them.

In-Depth Background:

Spiritual gifts are supernatural abilities given by the Holy Spirit to every believer. They are meant to build up the body, advance God's mission, and glorify Jesus. There are many types—teaching, serving, leading, encouraging, healing, and more—but all come from the same Spirit and are empowered by Him. Gifts are not the same as talents. While talents are natural abilities, spiritual gifts are empowered by God for spiritual purposes.

A Personal Example:

I remember talking with a man in our congregation who had been attending church faithfully for over a decade but never served. "I just don't have a gift," he told me. "I'm not a teacher or singer." But after taking a spiritual gifts inventory and talking through Romans 12 together, he discovered his gift was encouragement. It blew his mind—he had always been the one checking in on people, writing notes, and lifting spirits without realizing it was spiritual. "God gave me that?" he said. That realization changed everything.

Section 2: Goals of the Lesson

By the end of this lesson, students will:

1. Understand what spiritual gifts are and why they're given.
2. Recognize that every believer has spiritual gifts.
3. Learn the difference between gifts, talents, and fruit.
4. Be challenged to discover, develop, and deploy their gifts.

Section 3: Introduction Questions

What is a spiritual gift?

A Spirit-given ability to serve others and build up the Church.

Do all believers have spiritual gifts?

Yes. Every Christian is gifted by the Spirit for a unique purpose (1 Corinthians 12:7).

What's the difference between a gift and a talent?

A talent is a natural ability; a gift is a spiritual empowerment for ministry.

Section 4: Key Scriptures

1 Corinthians 12:4–7

There are different gifts, but the same Spirit distributes them.

- **Unity in Diversity** – Many gifts, one Spirit.
- **For the Common Good** – Gifts are not for spotlight—they're for service.
- **Gifted to Give** – Your gift exists to bless others.

Reflection Questions:

Q1. How does this passage challenge our view of competition or comparison in the Church?

Q2. What is one way your gift could serve others this week?

Romans 12:6–8

Paul lists several gifts and urges believers to use them.

- **Grace-Based Gifting** – We don't earn gifts—we receive them.
- **Exhortation to Action** – If you have a gift, use it.
- **Every Role Matters** – Teaching, giving, leading, serving—

all are equally valuable.

Reflection Questions:

Q1. Which of these gifts do you feel drawn to?

Q2. How are you currently using your gifts to serve?

1 Peter 4:10−11
Each should use whatever gift they've received to serve others.

- **Stewards of Grace** – Gifts are a form of God's grace.
- **Two Categories** – Speaking gifts and serving gifts—all empowered by God.
- **For God's Glory** – All gifts are meant to point people to Jesus.

Reflection Questions:

Q1. What does it mean to be a steward of God's grace through your gifts?

Q2. How can you serve in a way that glorifies God and not yourself?

Ephesians 4:11–13

Christ gave leaders to equip the saints for ministry.

- **Equipping and Building** – Leaders exist to help others use their gifts.
- **Body Maturity** – When everyone uses their gifts, the Church grows in unity.
- **Christlikeness Is the Goal** – Gifts aren't the end—they're the means to spiritual maturity.

Reflection Questions:

Q1. How have others equipped or encouraged you in using your gifts?

Q2. Who can you encourage to use their gift?

Section 5: Summary

The Holy Spirit gives every believer spiritual gifts to serve the Church, glorify Jesus, and help others grow. They are not spiritual status symbols—they are sacred assignments. You are not giftless. You are not unimportant. The Church needs what the Spirit has placed in you.

Don't bury your gift. Unwrap it, develop it, and use it for

God's glory.

Section 6: Application

- **Take a Gift Assessment** – Ask your pastor or leader for a spiritual gifts survey.
- **Serve Somewhere** – Gifts are discovered in motion.
- **Ask for Feedback** – Trusted mentors can affirm and clarify your giftings.

Daily Practices:

- Pray: "Holy Spirit, show me how You've gifted me."
- Step out in faith to serve—even if it's uncomfortable.
- Encourage someone else to identify and use their gift.

Section 7: Reflection Questions

What spiritual gifts do you think God has given you?

How are you actively using your gifts to serve others?

Who in your life can you help discover or develop their spiritual gifts?

Section 8: Prayer Prompt (ACTS Model)

Adoration – Holy Spirit, You are the giver of every good gift. You are generous, wise, and empowering.

Confession – Forgive me for ignoring or doubting the gift You've placed in me. Forgive my fear or complacency.

Thanksgiving – Thank You for uniquely gifting me and placing me in the body of Christ.

Supplication – Show me how to use my gifts. Give me opportunities, boldness, and humility to serve others for Your glory.

Example Prayer:

Holy Spirit, thank You for the gifts You've placed in me. Help me to stop hiding or hesitating. Teach me how to use my gifts to encourage others, strengthen the Church, and bring glory to Jesus. Make me bold and faithful in every opportunity You provide. Amen.

12

Lesson 11: The Guidance of the Holy Spirit

Key Truth:

The Holy Spirit doesn't just give directions—He walks the path with you.

Section 1: Introduction

Illustration:

Imagine going on a road trip in an unfamiliar city without GPS. You try reading road signs, glancing at a map, and following vague directions from strangers. Frustrating, right? Now imagine your GPS not only giving you directions but also driving the car. That's what the guidance of the Holy Spirit is like—He doesn't just point the way. He goes with you and within you.

Personal Connection:

Many Christians struggle to discern God's will. They ask, "What's next?" or "How do I know I'm making the right decision?" The answer isn't found in anxiety or guesswork—but in the presence of the Holy Spirit. He is your guide, counselor, and inner compass. This lesson will help you trust His direction in both big and small decisions.

In-Depth Background:

The Holy Spirit is described in Scripture as the "Spirit of Truth" who leads, teaches, and reminds us of what Jesus said. His guidance isn't mystical confusion—it's grounded in God's Word, confirmed by peace, and aligned with Christ's character. He leads us through Scripture, prayer, community, circumstances, and inner conviction.

A Personal Example:

A man in our men's group once shared that he was overwhelmed with a big career decision. He had two job offers—one with more money, and one that allowed him more time with his family and church. "I kept asking God to just tell me what to do," he said. But as he prayed, read Scripture, and talked with trusted believers, he realized the Spirit wasn't shouting from the clouds—He was guiding quietly through peace, conviction, and wise counsel. "The job with more family time gave me peace every time I prayed," he said. "That's when I realized the Spirit had been guiding me the whole time—I just needed to slow down and listen."

Section 2: Goals of the Lesson

By the end of this lesson, students will:

1. Understand the ways the Holy Spirit provides guidance.
2. Learn to recognize His voice and leading.
3. Discover how to walk in step with the Spirit daily.
4. Gain confidence in decision-making through spiritual discernment.

Section 3: Introduction Questions

How can I know if I'm being led by the Holy Spirit?

His guidance aligns with Scripture, produces peace, and reflects Christ's character.

What are some ways the Spirit speaks to us?

Through Scripture, inner conviction, godly counsel, prayer, and open or closed doors.

What does it mean to "walk in the Spirit"?

It means living with daily awareness, obedience, and sensitivity to the Spirit's voice.

Section 4: Key Scriptures

Romans 8:14
"All who are led by the Spirit of God are children of God."

- **Spirit-Led Identity** – Being led by the Spirit confirms you belong to God.
- **Relationship, Not Rules** – The Spirit doesn't bark orders— He walks with you.
- **Guidance as Assurance** – His direction is evidence of your salvation.

Reflection Questions:

Q1. How does Spirit-guided living strengthen your identity in Christ?

Q2. Where do you need the Spirit's leadership most right now?

John 16:13
The Spirit will guide you into all truth.

- **Truth-Based Guidance** – The Spirit never contradicts the

Word.
- **Glorifying Jesus** – He always points back to Christ.
- **Progressive Revelation** – He shows what we need when we need it.

Reflection Questions:

Q1. How does this verse reshape your understanding of God's guidance?

Q2. What does it mean to let the Spirit guide you into truth today?

Galatians 5:16, 25
Walk by the Spirit and keep in step with Him.

- **Ongoing Lifestyle** – Guidance isn't a one-time event.
- **Daily Alignment** – It's about walking with—not ahead or behind—the Spirit.
- **Flesh vs. Spirit** – Following Him means saying no to the old self.

Reflection Questions:

Q1. What helps you stay in step with the Spirit practically?

Q2. How can you tell when you've gotten out of step?

Isaiah 30:21

You'll hear a voice behind you saying, "This is the way. Walk in it."

- **Clear Direction** – The Spirit confirms your steps.
- **Personal Guidance** – He speaks to your situation, not just in general terms.
- **Course Correction** – When you drift, He brings you back.

Reflection Questions:

Q1. Have you ever sensed this kind of gentle redirection from God?

Q2. What's an area where you're asking Him, "Which way now?"

Section 5: Summary

God doesn't want you guessing. He's given you His Spirit to guide you. From major crossroads to daily decisions, the Spirit leads with clarity, peace, and truth. You don't have to figure it all out alone. You just have to stay close, listen, and trust.

The goal isn't just getting the right answer—it's walking with the right Guide.

Section 6: Application

- **Lean into Scripture** – God will never guide you contrary to His Word.
- **Listen for Peace** – The Spirit's guidance brings calm, not chaos.
- **Act in Obedience** – The more you follow, the clearer His voice becomes.

Daily Practices:

- Pray this each morning: "Holy Spirit, lead me today. Make me sensitive to Your direction."
- Journal your decisions and how you sense the Spirit's guidance.
- Spend 5 minutes in stillness asking: "What are You saying to me today?"

Section 7: Reflection Questions

What's one area where you need the Spirit's guidance right now?

How do you usually hear from God—and how can you grow in discernment?

What does it mean for you to trust the Spirit more than your own understanding?

Section 8: Prayer Prompt (ACTS Model)

Adoration – Holy Spirit, You are the perfect Guide. You are patient, wise, and faithful. I worship You as the One who leads me in truth.

Confession – Forgive me for rushing ahead or ignoring Your direction. Forgive me for leaning on my own understanding.

Thanksgiving – Thank You for always being present to lead, even when I don't listen the first time.

Supplication – Teach me to walk in step with You. Give me clarity in confusion, peace in waiting, and courage to follow.

Example Prayer:

Holy Spirit, I need Your guidance every day. I confess I've tried to lead myself and ended up lost. Help me walk in Your wisdom, stay close to Your voice, and trust that You're leading me even when the path isn't clear. Thank You for never leaving me to figure life out alone. Amen.

13

Lesson 12: The Power of the Holy Spirit

Key Truth:

The Holy Spirit's power isn't reserved for the spectacular—it's essential for everyday obedience.

Section 1: Introduction

Illustration:

Picture a lamp plugged into a wall outlet. It's well-designed, positioned perfectly, and built to give light—but until it's connected to power, it remains dark. The same is true for believers. Without the power of the Holy Spirit, we may look like Christians, but we lack the ability to shine. The Spirit doesn't just decorate your life—He empowers it.

Personal Connection:

Many believers live as if they're running on empty—frustrated, tired, and ineffective. But the Spirit has given us power—not just for ministry, but for life. This power isn't just for missionaries, pastors, or "super Christians." It's for you. It's for now. It's for everything.

In-Depth Background:

The Greek word for power (*dynamis*) refers to explosive, miraculous strength. But the Spirit's power isn't just for outward displays—it's for inner transformation, bold witness, persistent endurance, and overcoming sin. Jesus promised this power to every believer. The early church walked in it. So can you.

A Personal Example:

A retired pastor once told me that during one of the hardest seasons of his life—when his wife was going through cancer treatments—he had no strength left to preach, lead, or even pray some days. "But every Sunday," he said, "I stood in that pulpit and felt a strength that wasn't mine." He wasn't trying to impress anyone; he was just depending fully on the Spirit. "I didn't roar like a lion," he said. "But I didn't quit. That's the power of the Holy Spirit—not to make you superhuman, but to help you keep going when everything in you wants to stop."

Section 2: Goals of the Lesson

By the end of this lesson, students will:

1. Understand the biblical nature of the Spirit's power.

2. Recognize that power is not just for ministry, but for daily living.
3. Learn how to walk in spiritual strength and dependence.
4. Be encouraged to stop living by willpower and start living by Spirit power.

Section 3: Introduction Questions

What does it mean to live a Spirit-empowered life?

It means drawing strength, courage, and direction from the Holy Spirit rather than ourselves.

Is the power of the Spirit only for miracles?

No. It's also for resisting temptation, loving others, enduring hardship, and sharing the gospel.

Why do so many Christians feel powerless?

Because they rely on their own strength instead of the Spirit's.

Section 4: Key Scriptures

Acts 1:8

"You will receive power when the Holy Spirit comes upon you..."

- **Power with Purpose** – It's for boldness in sharing the gospel.
- **Personal and Global** – The Spirit works in you—and through you to reach others.
- **Empowered Witness** – The gospel advances by Spirit power, not charisma.

Reflection Questions:

Q1. Where do you need more boldness in your witness?

Q2. How can you depend on the Spirit in conversations with others?

Ephesians 3:16–17

Paul prays that we would be strengthened with power through the Spirit in our inner being.

- **Strength for the Soul** – The Spirit empowers from the inside out.
- **Rooted in Love** – Power isn't brute force—it's grounded in

love.
· **Prayerful Access** – Ask for this strength—it's available.

Reflection Questions:

Q1. What would it look like to be "strengthened with power" in your inner life?

Q2. How does Spirit-powered strength differ from willpower?

2 Timothy 1:7
"For God gave us a spirit not of fear but of power and love and self-control."

· **Power Over Fear** – The Spirit drives out fear.
· **Balanced Power** – It's paired with love and discipline.
· **Confidence in Calling** – Power makes you bold in your assignment.

Reflection Questions:

Q1. Where has fear held you back from obedience?

Q2. How does it help you face fear knowing the Spirit empowers you with strength, love, and self-control?

Romans 15:13

"...that you may abound in hope by the power of the Holy Spirit."

- **Hope Through Power** – The Spirit fuels enduring hope.
- **Overflowing Confidence** – You don't just survive—you abound.
- **Power for the Heart** – It's not just action—it's emotional and spiritual vitality.

Reflection Questions:

Q1. In what area of your life do you need the Spirit's power to hope again?

Q2. How can you let His power overflow into someone else's life this week?

Section 5: Summary

The Holy Spirit gives you the power you need for the life you're called to live. Not just for ministry—but for marriage. Not just for preaching—but for patience. Not just for mission trips—but for Monday mornings. You were never meant to live the Christian life alone.

Stop running on empty. Start walking in power.

Section 6: Application

- **Ask for Strength** – Daily surrender your weakness to the Spirit's strength.
- **Step into Boldness** – Don't wait to feel ready. Move in faith, trusting His power.
- **Fuel with the Word** – Power flows through truth—stay in Scripture.

Daily Practices:

- Start each day with this prayer: "Holy Spirit, fill me with power to live for You."
- Identify one area where you've been striving in your own strength—and invite the Spirit into it.
- Memorize 2 Timothy 1:7 and declare it when fear rises.

Section 7: Reflection Questions

Where are you relying on your own strength instead of the Spirit's?

How would your life look different if you truly walked in the Spirit's power?

What's one area where you need to ask for power right now?

Section 8: Prayer Prompt (ACTS Model)

Adoration – Holy Spirit, You are powerful, present, and limitless. I praise You as the strength of my life.

Confession – Forgive me for depending on my own energy, effort, and emotions instead of Your power.

Thanksgiving – Thank You for not only giving me salvation—but strength for every step.

Supplication – Fill me with power. Help me face today with Your boldness, not my fear. Use me beyond my limitations.

Example Prayer:

Holy Spirit, I am tired of living in my own strength. I need Your power to obey, to endure, and to overcome. Fill me. Strengthen me. Use me. Not for my glory, but for Yours. Let Your power be made perfect in my weakness. Amen.

14

Lesson 13: Walking in the Spirit

Key Truth:

Walking in the Spirit is not about perfection—it's about direction.

Section 1: Introduction

Illustration:

Imagine two people walking side by side on a trail. One listens, responds, and adjusts their steps to match the guide. The other keeps running ahead, lagging behind, or wandering off. Both are on the same path—but only one is walking in step. That's the difference the Holy Spirit makes when we choose to walk with Him, not just near Him.

Personal Connection:

Many Christians are frustrated with their walk because they're trying to run it alone. Walking in the Spirit isn't about trying harder—it's about staying close. The Spirit doesn't drag us forward; He invites us into a journey of obedience, trust, and alignment. This final lesson brings together everything we've learned and invites you to take it from knowledge to lifestyle.

In-Depth Background:

"Walking in the Spirit" is a New Testament phrase that implies continual, conscious dependence on the Holy Spirit. It involves yielding to His direction, resisting the desires of the flesh, and producing fruit that reflects the character of Christ. It's how believers grow, endure, and thrive—not by law, but by grace empowered through the Spirit.

A Personal Example:

A woman in our Bible study shared that for years she felt like a failure because she couldn't "live up" to what she thought a good Christian should be. Every time she messed up, she felt like she had to start her walk with God over from scratch. But when she finally understood that walking in the Spirit wasn't about being perfect, but being *willing to keep walking*, everything changed. "Now," she said, "I just ask Him to help me take the next right step. And when I fall, I don't hide—I reach out. That's what walking with Him looks like."

Section 2: Goals of the Lesson

By the end of this lesson, students will:

1. Understand what it means to walk in the Spirit daily.
2. Recognize the contrast between walking by the flesh and walking by the Spirit.
3. Learn how to stay in step with the Spirit in practical ways.
4. Commit to living a Spirit-led life beyond this study.

Section 3: Introduction Questions

What does it mean to walk in the Spirit?

It means living daily in dependence on and obedience to the Holy Spirit's leading.

How is this different from just believing in Jesus?

Walking is ongoing and active—it's how we grow, not just how we're saved.

Why is it important to stay in step with the Spirit?

Because He leads us toward life, truth, and transformation. The flesh leads us in the opposite direction.

Section 4: Key Scriptures

Galatians 5:16, 25
Walk by the Spirit... Keep in step with the Spirit.

- **Intentional Living** – Walking requires purpose and direction.
- **Conflict with the Flesh** – The Spirit and flesh oppose one another.
- **Step-by-Step Obedience** – This is a journey, not a sprint.

Reflection Questions:

Q1. Where in your life are you feeling the tension between flesh and Spirit?

Q2. What does "keeping in step" look like practically in your daily life?

Romans 8:5–6
Those who live according to the Spirit set their minds on the things of the Spirit.

- **Mindset Matters** – What we dwell on shapes how we walk.
- **Life and Peace** – The Spirit leads us to freedom, not fear.
- **Spirit-Led Focus** – Choosing where your thoughts go is part of walking in the Spirit.

Reflection Questions:

Q1. What thoughts have been shaping your direction lately?

Q2. How can you set your mind more intentionally on the Spirit?

Colossians 3:1–3
Set your hearts and minds on things above.

- **Spiritual Vision** – Walking with the Spirit involves lifting your eyes.
- **New Identity, New Focus** – You've been raised with Christ—now live like it.
- **Guarded Affections** – Walking well requires guarding what captures your heart.

Reflection Questions:

Q1. What is currently drawing your attention away from spiritual things?

Q2. How can you realign your heart and mind with the things of God?

Section 5: Summary

To walk in the Spirit is to live daily in step with God's presence, purpose, and power. It's the lifestyle of a believer who knows they can't do it alone and doesn't have to. When you choose Spirit-dependence over self-effort, you begin to experience the freedom and joy God designed for you.

The Spirit isn't just for your past salvation or your future eternity—He's for your next step.

Section 6: Application

- **Start Small** – Invite the Spirit into your next decision.
- **Check Your Steps** – Ask, "Am I keeping in step—or trying to lead?"
- **Stay Connected** – Prayer, Scripture, and obedience keep you in rhythm.

Daily Practices:

- Begin the day with: "Holy Spirit, lead my steps today."
- End the day with a review: "Where did I walk with You? Where did I drift?"

- Memorize Galatians 5:25 and repeat it when you feel spiritually out of step.

Section 7: Reflection Questions

How have you grown in your relationship with the Holy Spirit through this study?

What's one habit you can build to help you walk more closely with the Spirit?

How can you encourage others to join you in living a Spirit-led life?

Section 8: Prayer Prompt (ACTS Model)

Adoration – Holy Spirit, I praise You for being my constant guide, comforter, and friend. You are faithful in every step.

Confession – Forgive me for trying to live this life on my own. Forgive the times I've rushed ahead or resisted Your leading.

Thanksgiving – Thank You for walking with me. Thank You for the joy, peace, and strength You bring.

Supplication – Teach me to stay in step with You. Shape my thoughts, my actions, and my heart to reflect Yours.

Example Prayer:

Holy Spirit, help me walk with You today and every day. Don't let me run ahead or fall behind. When I stumble, help me rise. When I drift, call me back. May my life move in rhythm with Your voice and direction. Thank You for never leaving my side. Amen.

About the Author

Raymond Smith is the founder of *Disciple Blueprint*, a faith-based platform committed to helping believers grow deeper in their walk with Christ through Bible study, spiritual growth tools, and practical discipleship. With over four decades of leadership experience in the IT industry, Raymond now devotes his time to equipping others to live boldly for Jesus.

Saved at age six during Vacation Bible School and called to rededicate his life at 32, Raymond brings a personal, relatable touch to everything he writes. His teaching style is rooted in biblical truth, laced with clarity, authenticity, and the occasional touch of humor. Whether through his blog, Bible studies, or speaking, Raymond encourages Christians to grow in faith and boldly live out God's calling.

Raymond lives in Northwest Pennsylvania, where he enjoys

spending time with his niece and nephews, his two dogs—Penn and Riley—and investing in his local church community. *Empowered* is his first published Bible study, created to help everyday believers discover the life-changing presence and power of the Holy Spirit.

Email: raymond@discipleblueprint.com

You can connect with me on:
- https://www,discipleblueprint.com
- https://www.x.com/DbBlog
- https://www.facebook.com/discipleblueprint
- https://www.instagram.com/discipleblueprint

Subscribe to my newsletter:
- https://discipleblueprint.com/?ff_landing=4

www.ingramcontent.com/pod-product-compliance
Lightning Source LLC
Chambersburg PA
CBHW071522120626
46550CB00006B/2324